KU-207-682

# Looking After Your
# ·CAT·

# Looking After Your
# ·CAT·

· Edited by Ian Kearey ·

P
·PARRAGON·

First published in Great Britain in 1997 by
Parragon
Unit 13–17
Avonbridge Trading Estate
Atlantic Road
Avonmouth
Bristol BS11 9QD

ISBN: 0-7525-2161-6

Produced by Haldane Mason, London

*Acknowledgements*
Art Director: **Ron Samuels**
Design: **Digital Artworks Partnership Ltd**
Illustrations: **Robert Farnworth**
Picture Research: **Charles Dixon-Spain**

Printed in Italy

*Picture Acknowledgements*
All photographs by **Animals Unlimited**

Material in this book has previously appeared
in *The Complete Book of Cat Care* by Jane Oliver

# · CONTENTS ·

# Introduction

Cats are handsome, elegant animals with an independence of spirit that makes them fascinating and rewarding pets. Though they will never provide the slavish devotion of a dog, they are capable of deep attachment to an owner who understands their needs, and can provide many years of satisfying companionship. One of the most intriguing qualities of the cat is that only a thin veneer of domestication overlays its basic wildness, so that it can turn from a cuddly bundle of purring contentment into a savage hunter in a matter of minutes.

Over recent years, while the reputation of dogs has taken a knock, cats have gained in popularity. On a practical level they are clean, quiet, relatively undemanding, and they adapt just as easily to a tiny flat as to a country estate. It has even been demonstrated that cats are good for our health: the soothing action of stroking a cat lowers blood pressure and pulse rate and cuts the signs of damaging stress.

# Chapter 1

# A New Cat

$Y$our cat may be part of the family for the next 18 years, so a little planning in advance will ensure that you make the right choice.

*Children and cats often form a strong bond of love and trust.*

You may assume that you want a kitten: not only will it be cute and comical for the first few months, but you will be able to train it in your ways from the beginning. On the other hand, it will need a lot more attention and cost you more in veterinary fees than an adult cat.

A kitten may be a good choice if you already have other pets, as it will be seen as less of a threat and will readily accept its place in the household. However, if you have young children, an adult cat is a more sensible choice: it will be better able to avoid clumsy little feet, and toddlers are less likely to end up with scratches. A mature cat may take longer to settle in – though cats are very adaptable – but it will be better suited to an elderly owner, or a household where everyone is out at work during the day.

• *A new kitten will immediately charm all the family.*

# CAT COSTS

*Over its lifetime, a cat will cost you several thousands of pounds, so it makes sense to consider the costs involved before you buy. Take into account:*

- Initial outlay: bed, litter tray, feeding bowls, carrier.

- Food: reckon on at least a can of cat food each day.

- Litter: a 'must' for every cat, but if your cat is kept indoors, your litter expenses will be high.

- Neutering: more expensive for females than males.

- Vaccinations and annual boosters.

- Veterinary bills for sickness: an unknown quantity.

*As cats get older, be prepared for them to need more care and money spent.*

# Examining a kitten

• *The coat should be soft, smooth and glossy, with no tangles or matting. Part the fur and look for the tiny black specks that indicate flea infestation: fleas are more likely to be found under the chin, at the base of the spine and behind the ears. The ears should be clean and the inside should look slightly moist. There should be no red-brown wax visible in them.* •

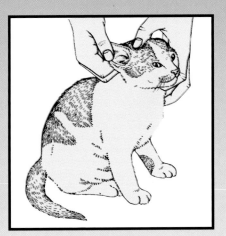

# CAT COLOURS

TABBY: covers a wide range of patterns and may be striped, spotted or ticked. It is the basic coat colour of the wild cat because it provides good camouflage in the countryside.

BLACK: considered lucky in Britain, unlucky in North America, black cats have a reputation for being 'difficult'.

WHITE: the dominant white gene may be linked to deafness, particularly in blue-eyed cats. White cats have delicate skin which may need protection from too much sunlight.

TORTOISESHELL: a mixture of black, yellow and orange. Almost always female, with the few males usually sterile.

GINGER: range from cream to reddish-orange, and because the underlying pattern of the coat is tabby, they are often striped. Gingers are usually male, and trainers report that they are the easiest cats to handle.

# Examining a kitten

- The mouth should be pink and clean, with no sign of soreness or inflammation and the teeth white. The body should be firm, and the ribs well-covered, with a slightly rounded abdomen, but no pot-belly. The eyes should be bright and clear – definitely not runny – and there should be no third eyelids (the little triangles of

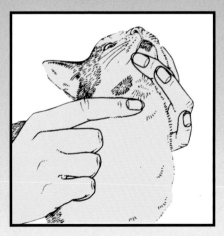

tissue at the inner corners of the eyes) showing. The nose should be velvety, cool and slightly damp. There should be no discharge or encrustation. •

# The first days

**A kitten should leave its mother only when it is fully weaned, at about eight weeks, and never earlier than six weeks. Bring it home when you are not too busy to give attention to the settling-in process. If possible, arrange to collect your kitten by car, and schedule the collection for well after a mealtime. Take details of the diet your kitten has been eating and only make any changes very gradually.**

Confine the newcomer to one room at first, providing a litter tray and a bed with a warm hot-water bottle tucked under the blanket. If you have other cats, this quarantine is essential, so that no germs are passed on. Wash and disinfect your hands each time you leave the newcomer.

A nervous kitten may hide in the most inaccessible spot it can find and refuse to eat. Put food down at each mealtime and leave the room so that the kitten feels it can venture out in safety. Follow much the same strategy with an older cat, uncertain about this new move.

# Basic equipment

**A small kitten will be comfortable in a cardboard box, with high sides for security and a door cut in the side. Line the box with several layers of newspaper, then a couple of old sweaters so that it can snuggle down and get used to your smell at the same time.**

Wicker baskets look attractive, but are difficult to keep clean. Plastic beds are hygienic and functional, and cosy 'igloos' with hooded tops are machine-washable. Some cats love bean bags, as they can knead them into shape. Sheepskin hammocks which hang on a radiator are appreciated by the sort of cats who insist on settling in the warmest place in the house.

Whichever bed you choose, it should be big enough to allow the cat to stretch out and should be placed in a quiet, draught-free spot.

Each cat must have its own feeding bowl. Pottery bowls are stable and easy to clean. Keep a special set of cutlery and can-opener for dealing with cat food, and wash all cat bowls separately from family dishes. A wide plastic mat over the feeding area is a good idea.

# KITTEN TIPS

- Always keep a kitten indoors until at least a week after its second vaccination.

- Never smack a kitten. It will not understand why you are punishing it and may learn to fear you.

- Always allow the new kitten enough sleeping time. Keep play sessions to five or ten minutes, then give the kitten time to calm down and rest.

*Small kittens are an appealing blend of independence and helplessness.*

- Never let a kitten (or a cat, for that matter) play with plastic bags; the risk of suffocation is too great.

- Always accustom your kitten to gentle grooming right from the beginning, so that it accepts this as part of normal routine.

# Housetraining

**Soon after a meal, a kitten will begin sniffing round for a suitable toilet area, so this is the moment to pick it up and place it in the litter tray. When a kitten squats anywhere but in the tray with its nose in the air, it should be speedily transferred to the tray.**

Keep the tray in the same place so that the kitten always knows where to find it, and site it in a quiet corner, away from feeding bowls. The most widely used cat litter is dried clay (Fuller's earth) which absorbs both moisture and smells. Wood-based litter is very absorbent and has a naturally pleasant smell. A washable litter is used with a specially designed tray which allows urine to pass straight through to another tray below, so that it can be emptied away.

Most cats will only use a clean tray, but this does not mean that you have to change the entire litter every day, or even every week. Scoop out wet litter and solid waste at least twice a day, and refill with new litter. Stand the tray on a piece of vinyl, which can be taken up and cleaned when necessary.

*Housetraining can begin on the first day a new kitten arrives in the home.*

# Chapter 2

# Food and Feeding

*C*ats are selective about what they eat and will usually inspect any meal offered very carefully before taking a mouthful.

*Smell and temperature are as important to them as taste, and their highly developed senses enable them to detect any slight loss of freshness not apparent to their owners.*

*They like variety in their diet and can become bored with the same food day after day, but their reputation as fussy eaters is much exaggerated.*

*When an owner reports that a cat will only eat smoked salmon and prawns or poached breast of chicken, it is usually because cats are very good at manipulating their owners. They are quite capable of sitting beside their untouched breakfast mewing hungrily for an hour, if they know that in the end something delicious will be provided.*

*Cats like food to be put in the same place, whether inside or outside the home.*

• *All cats retain their hunting instincts and need toys to let off steam.*

# Kittens

**Kittens have small stomachs, so they need feeding several times a day. From two to four months of age they should have four meat meals a day.**

There are proprietary brands of food specially formulated for kittens and, as a general rule, 200–300g (7–10oz) a day should be sufficient, but be guided by your kitten's appetite and don't worry if its sides bulge after a good meal.

You can provide variety by occasionally adding a little fresh meat or fish or cooked vegetables like carrot, cabbage or potato, finely chopped. The meat or fish should be cooked and never served raw.

At four months, reduce the number of meals to three, but feed a larger quantity each time, and at six months, move to the adult feeding pattern of two meals a day.

Establish a disciplined approach to eating by always serving food in the same place at the same time and by avoiding the pitfall of snacks between meals.

# FEEDING DO'S & DON'TS

*A kitten's inquisitive natures is one of its most appealing features.*

- Do serve all meals at room temperature, not straight from the refrigerator.

- Don't feed your cat snacks between meals.

- Do cook fish, poultry and pork; never serve them raw.

- Do feed your cat at a regular time and always in the same place.

- Don't serve food intended for dogs; it will not contain all the nutrients your cat needs.

*Cats should not be allowed to eat from humans' utensils.*

# Adults

**If the label states that it is a 'complete' food, canned cat food will cater for all the nutritional requirements of a healthy cat. An average amount would be eight heaped tablespoons a day.**

Feeding a cat entirely on home-cooked food is a tricky business, and you would need to use various supplements. It is easier, and more sensible, to provide variety in the diet by giving your cat fresh food two or three times a week. This might be beef, lamb or pork - with a sprinkling of carrots, green vegetables, or a little pasta - tinned sardines, tuna or mackerel, diced chicken with the skin left on, or white fish with a little cooked rice.

Dried food can be extremely useful, as it can be stored for longer and left down by owners who have to be away from home most of the day.

However, cats need to drink more water if they are on this type of diet, or urinary problems may result. Give a little dried food as an extra treat along with the normal diet.

• *Once weaned, kittens will enjoy the same foods as adult cats.*

# Drinking

**Cats are essentially desert animals, and can survive for a surprisingly long time without water.**

Under normal domestic circumstances, they absorb most of the fluid they need from their food and may seem to drink very little. However, your cat should always have access to fresh water, even if you never see it drinking. Don't use a tiny bowl, as cats like to drink from containers that are at least as wide as their whiskers.

There is nothing unusual about a cat preferring to drink from the birdbath, the fishpond or even a puddle – it seems that they offer more interesting smells than chemically treated tap water.

Some cats dislike the smell of freshly drawn tap water and will only drink after it has been standing for a while; others only like to drink from a running tap. Occasionally a cat will decide that the toilet offers the most palatable supply of water, but this should be discouraged by keeping the toilet lid closed.

Contrary to widespread belief, milk is not necessary to a cat's diet. Though cow's milk contains valuable nutrients, many cats cannot digest it and it gives them diarrhoea.

• *Although they are domesticated, cats are essentially outdoor animals.*

# Fussy cats

**There may be some good reason why your cat picks at its food: perhaps its food bowl is in a busy area, where it is disturbed, or it would prefer several small meals, rather than two substantial ones.**

When a cat paws the ground around its food, all it means is that the cat is not hungry enough to eat the food at the moment: in the wild it would cover up the food, and would return to it later.

If your cat refuses everything but some special delicacy, try putting things right by chopping the favourite food very finely and mixing it with a similarly flavoured canned cat food. If your cat refuses to eat it, leave it down for a reasonable length of time, then remove it.

Ignore all pleas and serve an identical meal next time. It will do your cat no harm to miss a few meals, and it will not allow itself to starve. Once it gets used to the new menu, cut down the amount of the special delicacy bit by bit.

• Cats often have their own favourite places in a home. If you feel you would not like you best sofa covered in cat hair, cover it with a blanket or counterpane, then remove it when you or your guests want to use the sofa. Your cat will not mind, and be encouraged to move on to less valuable pieces of furniture if it grows attached to the blanket.

# Chapter 3

# Understanding Your Cat

Cats have a reputation as aloof and independent, but most owners find that they develop a close understanding with their pets.

The more you talk to your cat, the more it comes to recognize and respond to your tone of voice – and the same is true the other way round.

Most domestic cats develop a range of miaows to signify their wants: the 'I'm hungry' miaow will be quite different from the 'let me out' miaow or the 'cuddle me' miaow. Besides miaowing, they may have a vocabulary ranging from teeth-clicking sounds to a blood-curdling howl .

Purring is usually associated with contentment and relaxation. As a general rule, the happier the cat, the rougher and louder the purr. As the cat becomes sleepy and prepares to settle down, the purr becomes softer and gentler, subsiding into a faint buzz.

*Cats will sleep anywhere, but appreciate having their own bed.*

• A happy kitten will grow up to be a contented cat.

# Body language

**The cat's body is very expressive, as it uses its eyes, ears, tail, posture and even its whiskers to show its feelings.**

The tail is a dependable barometer of a cat's mood. An upright tail means that the cat is friendly and confident, and a bend at the tip signifies real pleasure or happiness. If the tail is horizontal, the cat is unsure, and a dragging tail means that the cat is unhappy or unwell. A slowly wagging tail can signify alertness, anticipation or indecision, and a tail which thumps the ground repeatedly shows anger.

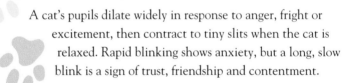

A cat's pupils dilate widely in response to anger, fright or excitement, then contract to tiny slits when the cat is relaxed. Rapid blinking shows anxiety, but a long, slow blink is a sign of trust, friendship and contentment.

When the cat is alert and pleased with life, its ears are pricked up and facing straight ahead; if it becomes annoyed, the ears pull back towards the side. Twitching ears may indicate that the cat is nervous.

When it is stalking, its ears sometimes flatten sideways, giving a clear 'do not disturb' signal.

• *A cat expresses happiness in every part of its body.*

# Territory

**The territorial instinct is very important for cats, as the size of the territory dictates the size of the food supply in the wild.**

Even a cat living entirely indoors does not lose this instinct, and if another cat wanders too near the window it may pound on the glass, yowling in fury, then run round the edge of the room, redefining the territorial boundaries.

Several cats sharing a home will usually hold their territory in common and defend it against outsiders, though one cat make stake a claim to a particular place and drive off others. Within the territory, a cat will have its favourite spots for sleeping and sunning itself, and probably a carefully selected vantage point for surveying the scene.

The cat will patrol the territory regularly, marking the boundaries with its scent by spraying, rubbing up against walls and fences, and scratching trees. Where the properties of various cats meet, there will be acknowledged areas where a number of cats will gather as part of their normal social life. A new cat often has to battle to assert claims to its own garden, which has previously formed part of another cat's territory.

# Hunting

• *When pursuing its prey a cat will first approach slowly and stealthily, then it will break into a crouching run, its body close to the ground, pausing then running forward again until it is close enough to take cover for the final pounce. It then stops, its eyes unwaveringly fixed on its quarry, its tail twitching in anticipation and its haunches moving to gather momentum. Finally it launches itself forward, leaps, and pins down the prey with its front paws.* •

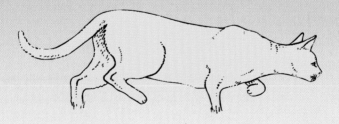

# Sleeping

**Like their wild cousins, domestic cats indulge in short bursts of activity in between long periods of rest.**

An adult cat sleeps about 16 hours a day – longer if there is no one at home and nothing to rouse its interest. It may well choose prime locations, such as your favourite armchair or your bed, but it may prefer a seemingly inhospitable, but warm, place like the top of the washing machine or video recorder.

Outside, it will usually choose a high place, well out of possible danger, and may even settle down for a quiet snooze while balanced on a narrow fence-top or wall.

More than two-thirds of the 16 hours is spent in 'napping' and the rest is deep sleep. A cat's brain waves retain much the same pattern as during waking times, which probably explains its ability to spring up in an instant, fully awake.

Presumably a cat's dreams mirror its waking experiences, and you may see twitching legs and ears and hear little mews of excitement or distress. If the dream is obviously turning into a nightmare, you can help the cat by waking it with a gentle touch and soothing words.

# Agility

- The unique agility of the cat is most obvious in the 'self-righting reflex' which comes into play the instant it feels itself falling. A complex organ in the cat's inner ear, called the vestibular apparatus, tells its brain its exact position in space. An automatic sequence of movement follows, with the cat first adjusting its head and then its body into the right position for a safe landing. •

# BEHAVIOUR PROBLEMS

Cats are much more trainable than many owners realize, and if behaviour problems do arise, they can often be dealt with quite simply, so long as you take the time to see the world from your cat's point of view. Cats love the safety of routine, and any change in their familiar surroundings or the behaviour of their owners can cause stress, which shows itself in various ways. Among the stress-bringing changes are:

- Guests in the house

- Death in the family

- Redecoration or new furniture

- A new baby

- The arrival of a new pet

- Marriage breakup

*Even if from the same household, cats can have territorial fights.*

• Opposite: *Cat toys are easy to make and cheap to buy.*

# Spraying

**Normally, cats do not feel the need to spray indoors, as there is no need to protect the territory against invaders, though when several cats share a house, each may mark out its own patch or territory.**

If your cat suddenly starts spraying, look for some change in the household that has put it under stress. You might try placing a tray of marbles below the spraying places, but a determined sprayer may simply stand further away. A sheet of household foil wrapped round chosen spot may work, as cats dislike the sound of urine spraying onto foil. The psychological approach may be more successful.

If you have more than two cats, try giving each one a separate room or separate place to sleep in. If your neighbour's cat is always prowling round outside and trying to slip in through the kitchen door, chase it away.

If you have installed a cat flap recently, try boarding it up and see if the behaviour stops. In difficult cases, confine the cat to one room when unsupervised, and make sure it has a cosy bed in a warm spot, perhaps under a radiator.

# Soiling

**Soiling may be caused by the same upsets as spraying, but it can also be the first sign of illness, so a veterinary checkup is advisable. Perhaps the cat has a bladder problem or is suffering from constipation, so that it has begun to associate the litter tray with pain and discomfort.**

In some cases the cat may be asking for the litter tray to be changed more often, or it may be unhappy with the type of litter used.

Never smack or scold a cat for soiling, even if you catch it in the act; this will increase any feelings of insecurity and make the behaviour worse.

Begin by cleaning the area thoroughly with a warm solution of biological detergent, followed by surgical spirit, or with a weak solution of household bleach, and a scattering of baking soda.

Don't use any disinfectant containing chlorine or ammonia; it may smell clean and fresh to you but to a cat it smells as though another cat has been in the house and draws it back to the place. Some disinfectants can also be absorbed through the paws.

# Scratching

**It is unusual for cats to be aggressive towards people unless they are unwisely handled, but they may develop the 'petting and biting syndrome'.**

One minute your cat is sitting quietly on your lap, purring and giving every appearance of enjoying your stroking hand, then the next minute it fastens its front claws into your hand and sinks its teeth into your flesh, while its back claws beat at your arm.

If this happens, limit yourself to short sessions of petting your cat for the time being. When it sits on your lap leave it free to get down as soon as it wants. After a few minutes, put it down.

Probably your cat will want to initiate more contact, and its moments of feeling under threat will become less frequent.

A cat that fastens its claws into your ankles every time you pass, pounces on your moving hand with claws outstretched or becomes overexcited in play and inflicts minor wounds, may not have enough action and stimulation in its life. If possible, give it more opportunity to go outside, even if you have to take it on a harness.

# Petting and biting

• *One minute your cat seems to be enjoying your caresses, and the next minute it has your fingers in a vice-like grip. This is playful, but be cautious. When it happens make sure the cat knows you are in pain. If the problem persists allow the cat on your lap until it starts biting you. As soon as the cat bites, put*

*it on the floor. Use this tactic and eventually the cat will stop biting because it will want to remain on your lap.* •

# Chapter 4

# Caring for Your Cat

Cats cost little in cash or effort compared to the pleasure they give their owners, but it is not sufficient to feed them and leave them to their own devices.

A little time spent catering to your cat's needs will pay dividends in producing a lively pet in peak condition.

Play is just as important for kittens as for children, as part of the learning process.

When kittens stalk and pounce on their mother's waving tail they are beginning to practise their hunting skills, and when they ambush their litter-mates, rolling over and over in mock combat, they are learning attack and self-defence.

Adult cats will keep a kitten's love of fun and games throughout their lives, so long as it is encouraged by their owners.

*Spend time playing with your cat – both of you will benefit.*

• *Kittens' curiosity can get them into all sorts of scrapes.*

# Playthings

**For scratching: out of doors, cats will usually find their own scratching places, but a good, solid log with bark intact will be appreciated. Inside, a scratching post is essential, otherwise your upholstery will soon be hanging in ribbons.**

There are plenty of commercially made posts available, but it is easy to make your own scratcher by gluing an off-cut of high quality carpet to a flat piece of wood, which is then fixed to the wall in a concealed corner, or even by wrapping sisal rope closely round a table leg. The rope or carpet can then be replaced as soon as it is worn.

For rolling and chasing: ping-pong balls, plastic lemons, wine corks, pine cones, catnip scented 'mice' from pet shops, pens and pencils to be batted onto hard flooring.

For jumping and pouncing: aluminium foil ball or feather on a string dangled in the air, dressing-gown cord or cotton reel on string pulled slowly along floor.

For ambush: strong paper bags, cardboard boxes, old blanket scrunched up in a heap.

# Cat flaps

**The most useful type of cat flap has a clear plastic door, so that the cat can see where it is going and what awaits on the other side, has a magnetic strip along the sides to keep out draughts and an either-way locking device.**

The lock means that you can fasten the door shut at night, allow the cat to come in but not go out, and vice versa. Check that the flap is easy to push and will not snap back too hard and trap a paw, and that it opens quickly to give the cat a speedy escape route from a trespassing dog.

*Although essentially solitary animals, cats enjoy each others' company.*

If there are other cats in the neighbourhood, you might prefer the type of flap activated by a magnetic collar so that it will only open for your own cat.

The flap should be fitted near enough to the base of the door for the cat to step through rather than jump. If this means that it is within an arm's reach of the door lock, fit a higher lock.

# Children and Cats

**Cats and children can get along very well together, providing the children are taught a few simple rules and never allowed to think of the cat as a cuddly toy to be squeezed and hauled about.**

Babies can be guided to stroke a cat with the flat of the palm.

Toddlers can be shown how to make friends with a cat, holding out a hand for the introductory sniff, then waiting for the cat to make friendly overtures before beginning to stroke and rub round its ears, along its back and at the base of the tail, leaving the tummy and back legs alone. They should understand that the cat must not be disturbed when it is eating, sleeping or using the litter tray.

It is probably best to teach young children not to pick up the cat at all as they usually hold a cat too tightly and hang on to it when it struggles. Some cats will put up with this kind of treatment, but most will protest vigorously, and your child may end up scratched or bitten.

# Grooming short-haired cats

• *Comb with a fine-toothed comb, starting round the head and under the chin, then working along from head to tail. Use a bristle brush to remove the dead hair, and stand the cat on its hindlegs to brush the chest and tummy. Rub with a chamois leather to bring out the shine of the coat.* •

# Collars

**A collar with an identity tag bearing your phone number will mean that your cat can be returned home if it roams too far, and that you can be notified immediately if it is injured in an accident.**

However, there is always the danger that the collar will get caught on a branch or fence and the cat will be unable to get free. For this reason, the collar should always have an elastic strip, to enable the cat to wriggle out, but even with this safeguard, many a cat has hanged itself on its collar.

You can minimize the risk by cutting part-way through the elastic so that it will break at any sharp tug, and be prepared to replace the collar often.

When fitting the collar, you should be able to insert one finger between the collar and the cat's neck. If there is room for two fingers, the collar is too loose.

# Grooming long-haired cats

• Start combing with a wide-toothed comb around the head and neck. Move to the legs, then raise the cat on its hind legs to comb the abdomen and the underparts of the 'trousers'. Once the wide-toothed comb goes through easily, change to a fine-toothed comb. Work along the back and sides, combing in an

upwards direction. Start at the hind end and work towards the head. Using a wire brush, brush the fur vigorously the 'wrong' way. •

# Trimming claws

• Use sharp clippers specially designed for the job; don't use ordinary scissors, which may splinter the claw. Press the pads of the paw gently, so that the claws are exposed. Cut only the white tips, which are dead tissue. Never touch the pink quick within the claw. Many cats never need to have their claws trimmed. If you are unsure about trimming the claws, ask your vet whether it is really necessary. •

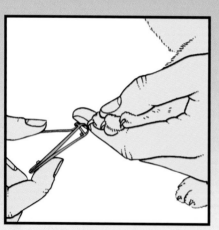

# Bathing

• Fill the sink or a large bowl with warm water, about blood heat, to a depth of about 10cm (4in). Lift in the cat and use the jug to wet its fur, starting from the back and ending at the neck. Once the fur is wet, gently massage in the shampoo, taking care not to let it near the ears or eyes. Keep rinsing with warm water until all traces of shampoo are gone. Gently clean round the cat's face with a soft, damp cloth. •

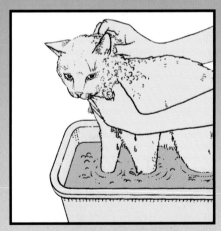

# Chapter 5

# Health Care

*C*ats may show few symptoms in the early stages of an illness, and in a busy household, these can be easily overlooked.

The secret of good cat care is knowing your pet's habits and keeping a close eye if they change in any way.

In an emergency, you will want to get your cat to the veterinarian as quickly as possible, but you may need to administer first aid in the meantime.

Never give your cat medicine meant for humans or other animals, and don't give an injured cat anything to eat or drink before seeing the veterinarian.

Remember that if it is frightened or in pain, your normally affectionate cat may turn on you and inflict injuries, so if possible wear a pair of gloves or have a coat or blanket ready to wrap round the cat if necessary.

*With a sensible approach, giving a cat treatment can be easy.*

• *Long-haired cats must be groomed regularly and thoroughly.*

# CHECKLISTS

*If you notice any of the following symptoms you should take your cat to the veterinarian immediately:*

• Excessive thirst.

• Marked changes in eating patterns: the cat is off its food or is eating much more than usual for more than 24 hours.

• Straining in the litter tray.

• Generally dull and listless appearance.

• Noticeable weight loss.

• Bleeding from the mouth, anus or genitals.

*Old cats love to sleep in the sun or other warm places.*

*Other symptoms may not be so clear-cut. Many a healthy cat will vomit or sneeze occasionally, without the need for a panic visit to the veterinarian. However, the golden rule is that if you are unhappy about your cat's condition or demeanour, contact the veterinarian without delay.*

# Visiting a vet

**In most areas, there is no shortage of veterinary surgeons, but not all veterinarians are equally good with all animals. Ask among local cat owners – or better still, cat breeders – to find the best cat veterinarian.**

When you first acquire your cat, take it along for a checkup, even if it does not need injections, so that the vet knows your cat and has its details recorded before you have to hurry along with a problem.

Ask whether he or she is willing to make house calls, if necessary, and what arrangements are made for 24-hour emergency cover.

When you take your cat for a consultation, note down any symptoms, any alteration in eating and drinking habits, anything unusual you have seen in the litter tray, and any marked changes in behaviour you have noticed.

The more information you can give, the easier it will be for the veterinarian to make an informed diagnosis.

# Nursing a sick cat

**A sick cat needs a quiet place in a warm, draught-free, but well-ventilated location.**

A large, high-sided cardboard box with a 'door' cut in the front will provide a snug bed, which can be replaced as often as necessary. Line the box with newspaper and towels, and provide a lukewarm hot-water bottle, carefully wrapped, in one corner.

Your cat may not be interested in eating, but tempt it with small, frequent meals of cooked fish or poultry, scrambled egg or meat and fish-based baby foods, and serve food warmed to blood temperature. Though a cat can go without food for quite a long time, dehydration can be a problem, and can become dangerous if the cat is losing fluid through vomiting and diarrhoea.

While your cat is sick, you may need to keep its face clean by wiping away any discharge from around the eyes, nose or mouth. Use a clean pad of cotton wool, dampened with fresh warm water, for each area. If there is diarrhoea, you will need to clean its rear end as well.

# Wrapping a cat

• Cats are notoriously difficult to hold in position for examination or treatment; they can wriggle, squirm and kick their way free if not held in the right way. Hold the cat by the shoulders, with one hand on each side of the body. Place the cat on a thick towel or small blanket, and wrap tightly. Tuck in the edge of the towel, leaving the head free ready for treatment. •

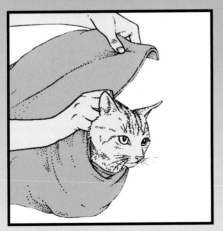

# SCRATCHING

## What to check

Are there black specks visible in the cat's fur?

Is there any sign of dry, scaly patches?

Are there any bald patches?

Do you live in the country? If so, check for small, bluish swellings.

Is the cat scratching its ears? Is there any dark brown wax visible?

## What to do

Use flea powder or spray: follow manufacturer's instructions exactly.

Consult your veterinarian immediately.

Your cat probably has a skin disorder.

These are probably sheep ticks. Ask your vet to remove them; partial removal can lead to abscesses.

Ear mites are very common; your veterinarian will prescribe ear drops.

# Giving a pill

• Place your left hand over the cat's temples and raise its head slightly, pressing its jaws gently with your thumb and index finger. With the index finger of your right hand, press lightly on the front of the cat's mouth to open it. Put the pill at the base of the cat's tongue and give it a slight push. Close the cat's mouth; if it does not swallow immediately, keep its head back and stroke its throat until it swallows. •

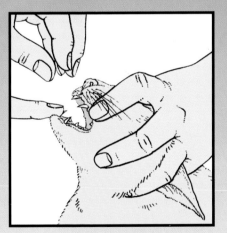

# FIRST-AID KIT

*Some minor injuries, such as flesh wounds or even choking, can be treated by the owner, but the golden rule is to consult a veterinarian as soon as the immediate danger has passed. If you are in any doubt about the cat's condition, ring the veterinary surgery right away and outline the symptoms clearly; the staff will advise you whether an early appointment is necessary.*

- Thermometer

- Safe disinfectant

- Blunt-ended scissors

- Tweezers

- Gauze pads

- Cotton wool and buds

- Bandages

*Always work gently and methodically when trimming cat's claws.*

- Antiseptic cream, specially formulated for cats

- Petroleum jelly

# Administering eardrops

• Clean dirt and wax from the outer folds of the ear with damp cotton wool, but don't attempt to poke inside. Hold the outer ear flap back and tilt the cat's head slightly sideways. Allow the liquid to drip into the ear canal, and hold the head steady for long enough to allow the liquid to penetrate. Gently massage the cat's ear, then clean away any excess liquid. •

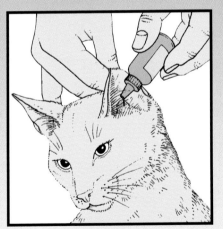

# Administering eyedrops

• When applying eye drops or ointment, hold the
cat's head steady with a hand across the temples, but
do not tilt it backwards. Drops should be applied from
above; ointment should be applied so that a small
amount falls across the eyeball. Hold the
eyelids together for a few moments before you
release the cat. •

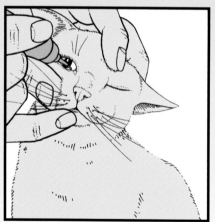

# Taking a temperature

This is a two-person job. Ask your helper to hold the cat by the scruff of the neck, with another hand under the body, behind the hind legs.

Use a small-bulbed clinical thermometer, the end greased with vegetable oil, and shake down the mercury.

Lift the cat's tail and insert the thermometer slowly but firmly into the cat's rectum, until about one-third is inside the cat.

Hold it in place for one minute, then remove and wipe it before reading. Normal temperature varies between 38° and 39°C (100° and 102°F).

If the temperature is higher or lower than these extremes, consult your veterinarian.

# Index

Page numbers in *italic* refer to illustrations